ROGUE APOSTLE

ROGUE APOSTLE

mary jane nealon

four way books
new york

Editorial Office
Four Way Books
PO Box 535
Village Station
New York, NY 10014
www.fourwaybooks.com

Library of Congress
Catalog Card Number: 00 134378

ISBN 1-884800-31-9

Linoleum Block Print by Catherine Nealon, *Johnny*
Book Design: Brunel

This book is manufactured in the United States of America
and printed on acid-free paper.

Four Way Books is a division of Friends of Writers, Inc.,
a Vermont-based not-for-profit organization. We are grateful
for the assistance we receive from individual donors
and private foundations.

ACKNOWLEDGMENTS

I would like to thank the editors of the following magazines in which some of these poems have been published in one form or another:

Chiron Review: "Facing the Wrong Way and Speeding"
The Kenyon Review: "The Ship Under the Foot of the Elephant," "Tagged"
Mediphors: "Your Suicide"
Mid-American Review: "The Chaos in Warrensburg, Missouri"
Things Shaped in Passing: More 'Poets for Life' Writing From the AIDS Pandemic (Persea Books 1997): "The Illustrious Providence of Solid Tumors," "The Pathologist Dictates," and "Watching the Solar Eclipse with AIDS Patients in Infectious Disease Clinic: May 10, 1994"

Grateful acknowledgment to The Fine Arts Work Center in Provincetown, The New Jersey State Council on the Arts, and the Mid-Atlantic Arts Foundation for their generous support. To Sally Ellsworth, whose generosity allowed for so many magical Septembers.

Thanks to Martha Rhodes for her smart editing, and to my teachers: Roland Flint, J. D. McClatchy, Steve Orlen, Daniel Tobin, and Jean Valentine. Thank you to Tom Sleigh for his thoughtful read. And finally, to Lee Briccetti, Priscilla Ellsworth, Victoria Hallerman, Wendy Wilder Larsen, Sabra Loomis, Myra Shapiro, and Susan Sindall, for decades of reading and writing together.

for my father who listened
in memory of my brother, John Patrick Nealon, Jr.
and my mother, Margaret Hourigan Nealon

CONTENTS

BODY PRISON

It is its own awful mystery.
She loses the brother, and with his body
that she loves so much, tumbles
with, washes; the bones of her own
shape dissolve. She holds onto
the bars of her ribs, longs to remember solidity.
She looks out past the bloody pulse of her heart.
Sees she is trapped.

In the long run, it is less about her body
than about a fear which rises inside her.
It is about imprisonment.
The way Earth keeps her, holds her back.

Look how empty her hands are now,
the same cracked leather of mitt
where she pounds and molds the center.
These ribs, these bars, wide enough for air
and not much else. She wants the brother's
hands, his long body, but God has taken it
with His tongue, with His immortal judgement:
who lives who dies.

I

The darkness is not hidden from itself.

—Bernard of Clairvaux

NIGHT SHIFT AT TERREBONNE GENERAL HOSPITAL: HOUMA, LOUISIANA

We are flying nurses living in a swampy
cul-de-sac behind the redneck bar.
Sheriff's deputies play cards
in our bedrooms while we sleep.
Hello little girl, they say, when I wake
at four in the afternoon.

In the kitchen sink, fresh grey shrimp
float in buckets. Duane, who owns
a double trailer home, will come back later
with spices, to cook for us.

Insects work my skin,
tearing back the salted first layer.

Fungus settles on wood beams,
under our toes.

A girl is raped, beaten and left on a hill.
Fire ants crawl across bruises,
stinging her even after she is dead.

Offshore, oil rigs work their dangerous machines.
Men lose hands or parts of hands.

Look in the mirror and blur your eyes.
Imagine the shimmering unclear outline you see
is your life. It is the way your life
will always be. The air even tastes like this.

WATCHING THE SOLAR ECLIPSE WITH AIDS PATIENTS IN INFECTIOUS DISEASE CLINIC, MAY 10, 1994

To save our retinas, we slip your x-rays from the film jacket.
Your entire radiographic history is here.
We choose the most recent picture of your chest,
the one with dense patchy infiltrates,
the one where, having failed to remove your gold chain,
a small cross is suspended among rib bones.

We line up, take turns passing the protective
slice of film back and forth. At the moment
when the moon pauses at the center of the sun
it has the same heavy black nucleus as the virus.
The ordinary slides out of sight.

Soon the drama has passed, the moon edging
its way along. We are tired of the way
death has waited. It lays its meticulous hand
on the young man with tall stalks of heliconia
across his knees, tulips for all of us in his arms.

DREAM OF SERVITUDE

What difference does your spine make now?

I am a rogue apostle
come to serve you.

I make a wig of red hair for the doll
you want, search the meadow
for eyes, a mouth, a nose.

This is nothing to ask for really,
not when your body is dissolving,
your soul ascending.

THE ILLUSTRIOUS PROVIDENCE OF SOLID TUMORS

...James Sauderling's mother tould him that she bewitched her Cow,
but afterwards said that her Cow should doe well againe, for it was
not her Cow but another person's that should dye.

—Transcript, Salem Witchcraft Trials

On the expensive SONY screen, cell clusters are zinnias.
Erratic tumor cells sliced down like this
astound us with their beauty. The pathologist sits up straight,
explains what will happen. I try to hold on to the idea
of your body: pierced nipples permanently erect,
a dangling half-moon in silver;
your well-loved rectum, your soft testicle sac.
Even when he focuses and zooms the slide,
nothing in this clump of tissue is evocative of you.

I think about the old witch woman,
taking a curse from this cow, putting it on another.
How they *boyled the Heart of a Calfe that Dyed, boyled*
the flesh, boyled the bones.
They weighed the bulk of things.
Large meaty pieces of disease.
They took the organs out, even after death,
to cleanse them. This they did by candlelight,
with much twisting of tongues, fits and raising-up.

We take the smallest parts of you: slice and split,
stain, enlarge. We muse over you.
No one will say AIDS, they imagine your cancer
as a separate and pure aberration. We talk of chemo
as though it were the ordinary course of things,
ignore the devastated slack face of your lover
who zips and unzips the leather jacket pocket,
who twirls the beautiful emerald
in your left earlobe with his long ring finger.

YOUR SUICIDE

for Howard

Your mother tells us about the note
you left on the motel room door
for the police: *I'm HIV positive,*
it said. *Please be careful.*

NIGHT SWEATS

The skin grows and stretches.
When peeled back,
bone shines white
and releases secrets.

Cells make circles of flame
to keep out the uninvited guest
who latches onto protein stems
or pockets of memory.

Hair grows and sheds on the pillow.
The eyes sit in their waxy coat,
undefined, light barely crosses
the threshold of cornea and lens.

This poor body and companion of body,
fear has penetrated all thought,
all gestures are gestures of *seeking*
and every evening, a storm.

TAGGED

Your husband recreates the picnic:
your artless splashing and one long
under-water dive into pond water,
(where parasites hook into nostrils,
travel the short distance to your brain).

I ticket you with your name and date of birth
while in the hall your husband huddles with your children.
He later does what no one else does, demands to see you
in the morgue, demands you be unraveled
so he can check the spelling on your toe marker.
He and I alone in the basement with your nude body.

Asleep in the lounge,
your children have already begun dreams
where they are sucked into dark water,
where tagged creatures wash ashore.
They feel,
in the sphere of sleep:
a small revenge,
a small recognition.

THE PATHOLOGIST DICTATES

On the phone to the morgue
I rattle off a list of cultures
we want from your abandoned body:
cryptococcus, toxoplasmosis, aspergillosis.

In the background the pathologist says,
in the most delicate of voices:
Now I am entering the bronchial tree.

All day I imagine this journey,
a black-bottom pool,
above me branches mirror our lungs.

In death, no collapsing
of the final breath,
rather a *holding-on* of air
beneath relaxed
and suspended chest muscles.

When we turn your body,
our careful movements shift
the last air in your bronchioles,–
small sounds:
a timid and unsure singing.

MOTORCYCLE ACCIDENT, NEW MEXICO

When the fender of the Buick takes your leg,
it takes it at the hip. A *disarticulation* we call it.
All the leg, including the round ball of femur
that fits into the smooth hip joint.

You are my age, with my hair, my coloring.
Because we have no way to close the wound
in the Emergency Room, and because it will take
some time to prepare the OR, I have my gloves

in balls of sterile gauze, shoved into the hole.
You drift in and out. My latex hands soaked in your blood.
Once you rouse and say, *my leg must be bad*
it hurts so much...broken, isn't it?

Later that night I saw your leg on a gurney in the morgue.
Tan, a torn ankle sock, blanched veins behind the knee.
Even though the nightmares when they come, are selfish:
my legs mangled, *I'm* running from the wolves,

it is the feel of my fist in your socket in your bone pocket,
hard place of intimate pressing to save your life, it is *that* sensation,
a kind of traumatic marriage that I wake to 14 years later,
my fist asleep, my neck stiff, just the way it felt

leaning into your body then. So when I do wake
in September of this year, warm rain like spots of your
blood on my forearm, I think about your split body,
craggy, torn, the strange love I had for you.

Fragile skin, hefty bone that separates, then gathers us
to rescue one another, what my life has come to,
the salvation of cornea and limb,
my hands, *emancipated* in the mess of it.

THE SOUL IN THE BURDENED LIMBS

She places a cool cotton cloth on the forehead of her son.
His small legs fall away from the center of his body.

It is the day Kin Moy will die and his mother has noticed
a change to his breathing. She is screaming

and we are without translators so I grab her hands, speak
sing-song, tell Kin Moy things I couldn't possibly know:

how beautiful it will be, how much he will love where he is going.
She watches and calms herself for him, her hands smooth

up and down his legs, a rapid Mandarin lullaby to move him
from this room into the air above the city, above

the vegetable market where someone has just found
his father, above the Second Grade classroom

where his brother is copying new English words
into his notebook. His soul left his thigh bones then,

left his delicate structured spine. I felt light shift,
felt grief transfer us all

to a place on the pillow
just above this child's head.

JUSTIFIABLE CIRCLES

Studio of glass boxes: mounted
and stacked: memory of skin
and vulnerable breath
caught in these transparent squares
(sharp-edged dripping glue).

Room here for lungs
which have forgotten their lung-work,
bone fragments to aid those
who have difficulty walking.

Glass boxes of memory: pieces of skin
paled eggshell white, sallow boxes.
Bitter taste of cardamom and ruin.
Glass boxes like autopsy jars:
wreckage of tissue and bone.
We are like this in our work:
wanting to save lives,
wanting to squash them.

I know that you are drawn-up
in the fetal pose of *suffering,*
your lymph nodes expanding soft groin skin
and underarm flesh, I know *that*
and still I stand here
for an hour watching thin white circles
overlap and intersect on the studio wall.
I think: *I can't go back there,* think
how do I stay in the smallest drawn circle?

I want to return this vision of you to you.
I want to offer up the images you left
when I wasn't looking
when I said *tell me your story*
when I was careless enough to think
I could change the way you endured it all
careless enough to think I could enter your room:
the glass box where you tossed and turned.

THE SHIP UNDER THE FOOT OF THE ELEPHANT

This thick-skinned toe scraping.
This cool cool water splashing upside down.

Breath, once so unconsciously available,
hides now in the shadow of the foot.

This moment of slow sinking into the waves,
this steady forcing down into green:

some panic, some music from the band
and the long soft hand of the nurse

who adjusts the morphine drip, just enough,
just to ease the weight of the elephant

and expand the idea
of where the ship might go.

II

He asked me to tell them that he had not breath
enough to frame his words and was too tired
to attend to anything, which I did,
not without tears.

—Alfred of Rievaulx

THE DIXON PENCIL COMPANY, 1963

We left the third-grade classroom
at St. Mary's and walked eight blocks
without coats or mittens
three days before Christmas to sing carols.
Plastic holly pinned just above our hearts.
The men outside Rivera's Wonder Bar
smiled and adjusted their crotches.
We held hands and walked two by two.
Our songs were bound
by red construction paper and green ribbon.
We couldn't stop,
even to pull up our knee socks.
When we got there, the workers
leaned over the railing and listened,
shuffled sawdust from the metal walkway,
picked blisters on their palms, their coughs
were deep, mysterious, and smelled of eggs.
This was long before I knew anything of despair.
Afterwards, they passed out Kool-Aid
in thin paper cups, gave us gift boxes–
newly sharpened pencils, some color, some lead.
Wood shavings flew around them in the air.

FACING THE WRONG WAY AND SPEEDING

More and more I am six.
My parents lose their patience.
I have everything I want: books, Beatle records,
multi-colored hair ribbons. A guitar.
And a music teacher named Mario
who slides his finger up under my tight
belted navy blue uniform while I count
three-quarter time and half time. Just rests it there,
not far up, at the edge of my white cotton undies,
his index tip. Just there. For one hour.
My father can't understand how it is possible
to have lessons for so long and not know any songs.

YEATS REVEALS IT

They line-up, line-up
at the fence and the great
craxen gaze down, their
great craxen eyes gaze
down-o and they line up
gazing down, their eyes
like peas gazing down
and if a small child
with all its moo-sounds
cannot outlive cancer, How
might I Cow? How might I?

SEQUESTERED

She stood alone in her room,
hands extended in the poses of Saints.
Something convinced her that weeds
would turn to roses with drooped and dewy petals.
On her bedroom door: a white tulle dress in plastic.

At Church, she practiced receiving the host,
the body and blood of Christ; the wafer stuck
to her palate, made her gag. She worked it
forward with her tongue and spit it out.
For punishment, she was forced to kneel

before the life-sized crucified Jesus. His perfect wax
features in agony, blood on both palms, on the arch
of his feet. She knew, at six, the burden of the spear.
Her small hand cramped from the weight of it
while the Cathedral's vacuous air

settled like a thrombus in her heart.
Only lately she remembers the poetry:
Mea Culpa, Mea Culpa, Mea Maxima Culpa,
the heavy gowns of the Saint and the beautiful
serpent, curled, *rapturous* at her feet.

HER FATHER MUST BE A SKYWRITER

Her hair color was inconsequential
except that it was his cast.
She lived, always looking up,
waiting for his love to spew out a frothy clue.

There was no foolishness.
He pulled the lever to release foam,
turning or dipping to make a word.
To her it was gospel. The book of him.

The stories he told, she inhaled as air.
He took all the lessons about pain, loss,
great art: spelled them out carefully for her
against the edge of the world.

SEIZING LIGHT

1969. Under bed covers, my brother and I
pressed our faces against a glass jar
of lightening bugs, captured beneath the tight lid:
jade globes of flicker, small glow
in our miserly hands. *What we wished for:*
to keep the power of flare and pause.
Driven as we were by ownership,
we let them escape into a cave of tented sheets
where we plucked *twinkle*
from the wedged connection of back and leg,
until we had, on our fingers, rings of fire
and a bed full of dead insects,
small wings flat and wet as hair.

*

1996. Four boys share fierce hard-ons
for scattered geese: Domesticated Snow,
brazenly white, a neighbor's venerable pets.
Power of strangling in their bare hands,
for the hefty flesh and feather.
In music, imitation and repetition,
and then the quandary of how to finish,
until all the energy builds and explodes.
Boys, birds. It happens.
A seven-year-old child sees,
in a puppet show, Punch strangle the devil,
and suffocates the new baby.

Pyromaniacs cluster their fires,
each building on the frenzied flame of the other,
so *these* boys start out, rage at their life, *small town:*
bloody fishermen on the docks doing heroin,
pissing on small cuts their hooks make,
circle of rumor and alcoholism and battering,
so they start out, take hold of the backs of geese,
each boy needing to out-do the other, how easy it is
to strangle the stupid birds, waddling, not flying away,
stopping only when one boy takes the stretched neck
in his mouth and tears the flesh between his teeth,
until, head and bill completely severed,
their ghastly fugue ends.

*

1969. The men have just landed on the moon,
and in a desperate attempt to fly
and understand gravity we take Victor Siegel's cat
to the roof of the Buckingham Hotel,
and spin it out and up, hearing a cat
always lands on its feet, but wanting,
each of us, for it to cleave and split.
When it doesn't, but thuds and runs away,
we go night swimming at Norwood Beach.
We have been forbidden this treacherous pleasure:
black night, waves invisible until they crash over us,
we slam into the black jetty, and eventually,
lungs seared from salt water, legs bruised, we give up.
The edge that night remains the edge, we skirt the fringe.
Our wet bodies disguise their disappointment.
In two days, Denny Diaz will drown at Sylvania Beach
and his mother's wide howl will alter us forever,

but for now, we head home, catch fireflies,
and with what is custom more than anything,
rip their green lights from them and fix them to our hands.

BAT BOX

For the child, the overstuffed chair
was a box for her hibernation.
She pressed herself into deep cushions,
let saltines melt in her mouth
for the sensation of salt and bread alone.

All around the bat child in dark
where she roosted and folded her wings:
the summer current and flaming sun.
She inched back out of sight until dusk,
when she flapped her heart open.

At night she would wake: *nattbakka:* origin
of her *self:* extravagant membrane of her nose,
of her clear extended ears. Sharp. Aware of everything,
but cloistered, she quivered in her dreaming
body: of *communion,* of *gathering.*

RIOT

By the summer of '68 I had only climbed two trees:
the elm on Erie Street and the dogwood in our backyard.
Someone wanted me to hate Puerto Ricans.
It wasn't my father, though he might have,
weighed down by riot gear, torched houses, bedlam.
It wasn't Juan from the bodega who sold three-day-old milk
and fancy flamenco dolls in tulle skirts.
It wasn't Tony, the vegetable man, who loved his asparagus
as much as his wife, who taught us, in detail, the complexities
  of the crop.
I bled in my quilted robe.
Castro was spotted on Montgomery Street by the Cubans.
I had a pink crushed velvet skirt, a tight ass,
and a Time Tunnel View-Master set.
Manuel Tirado, in his strawberry T-shirt and cut-off shorts
pressed his pelvis against me while we leaned
on my father's car, waiting for curfew.
I stopped wanting to *be* Evelyn Gonzalez.
I kissed Manuel and when he kissed me back,
I felt his tongue slide behind my teeth.
There were riots everywhere that summer,
but I only wanted the hot breath
of Manny's mouth:
Maria Juana, sus ojos, sus ojos.

IMAGINE YOUR FACE IS IN A MELON

Imagine your face is in a melon
and it is summer and nothing has happened all day
except you went to the Office Bar
in Farmington, New Mexico
and the really tall blonde guy
remembered that once you wore a white dress
with a picture of a Saint pinned to the collar

imagine your face is in his back
and his back is scarred with tar burns
from the mines,
your mind gets weak
from the sweet mud on his boots
and the rigid thumb joint
he pokes you with everywhere

it is summer
and nothing much is happening
you are nineteen
and your brother is dying so the bodies of men
fascinate you
this is what he will not have
you say over and over to yourself
as you settle into the soft curve
of pubis and bone

imagine your face is in a melon
and you are almost hysterical
the man you are lying with

has a cast on his leg
which opened the skin on your shin
with his banging love

imagine the torn fibers
he will never have
and loose seeds of melon *this*
your face is in it
and you can't breathe it is so ripe.

THE TRUTH ABOUT MYSELF

I cannot let go the brother's body from memory
where it rises in the mirrored image of my face.

I live in the wood knot's tight beginning,
in the tumor that devoured him.

To understand only, to query. *Wonderment*
stitched itself to my skin: won't let go of me.

HEART TASK

I'm cooking the sac of my heart
until it stops obsessing about beating.
Flub-flub, flub-flub and so on.
I want to sever its connection
to the rest of me, limit the nerves
snaking into my larynx and the soft
tissue of my neck.

I'm dissecting and embroidering
a new one, one that floats suspended
in deep breath, one that manages
to take a back seat to my kidneys
and fabulous spleen. My spleen
which has gone on quietly
making new spleens: pea-sized,
plum-sized and corpuscle-rich.

On the chest x-ray, in the landscape
of rib, a hole where my wide heart was.
Free air in the liberated space.
Room for fish in there.
A predator flies over, a vigorous hawk.
I toss my heart up in the air.
See it for what it is: a wall, a big question.

FARMINGTON, NEW MEXICO

I leave my body freely, enter your mouth's dark grotto.
My legs will only go so far, the sky stops them,
and the dome of tent stops them.
I pretend you do nothing for a living
except haul me to the moist plastic tent floor.
We roll in the foolish tent at the edge of the San Juan,
below your fifth rib and your nipple
is a halo of thick skin where branding irons scorched it.
I know when you shovel the Site,
slinging mud across exposed pipes and weeds
you are thinking of me. You are thinking
how *impossible* it is.

THE CHAOS IN WARRENSBURG, MISSOURI

How like fences we were once:
long beams of ourselves laid out
sturdy beside each other, while inside,
our hearts, untroubled, would bend
and brush against each other
the way grasses genuflect in wind.

It was quiet.
As quiet as the land dipping down
upon itself, or cows, the way they knelt,
disinterested. We walked around this place
where you were born, but I could not get in.
You understand this sparseness.
I understand storms, the way love moves
within them. I am comforted by thunder
and the slapping of trees across our walls.

I find it easy to love in small places:
tents: cramped caves where we huddle
from snow. This is *too much*
to hold hands and watch nothing happen.

Others see a peaceful house with a path
from the door, purple and red wildflowers,
and a fence, to hold the farm's passion inside.
I see a woman who comes to the back door,
throws her arms up to scare crows,
and the crows, glossy black pieces of bird,

fly off in opposite directions, then return,
a chaotic circle of seeds and birds.

I understand the places I cannot go to,
and the hard grinding sound a hinged gate makes
when it closes on itself.

THE CLARITY OF DUTY

The executioner loves me with calm blue eyes.
He lays the knotted rope with all its hemp
over the bridge my collarbone makes.

Witnesses have bitten the inside of their mouths.
But I love the one who kills me. The privacy
of his canvas hood the only thing between us.

Villagers lean on each other.
It is almost too much to bear.
One of the women sways and faints.

Everyone watches from the village square
and imagines what I want: strong rope,
a quick drop, a stallion come to save me.

III

What we have reached out towards is way above us, and we fall far short.

—Amedeus of Lausanne

UNINVITED GUEST

At the undertaker's house,
our mother, a teacher
of bilingual children from Guatemala

and Peru, lies back obediently
in pearl-grey metal, faith beads
folded in her hands.

The derelict pretends, at this wake
for sufferers and sorrow-makers,
to know us, so that afterwards

we will pass him whiskey, grateful
for his trembling condolences.
His race track form, fallen

from his pocket, suggests
he is a dreamer of *endings,*
like us.

WASHING DISHES, 1968

We are in the kitchen, my mother's bee-hive hair
so high it tilts and slides. Her worn dishtowel
fans out, her heels kick up and slap.
Coal dust from the furnace makes small powdery clouds.

We drop our knives and forks into given spaces,
and dance for each other on the ruddy tiled floor.
My aunt Anne repairs the oven's hinge with Band-Aids,
scoops coal from the scuttle with a flat-mouthed shovel.

The kettle whistles, suds go flat, all our ankles
have the wide silhouette of cooks and chamber maids.
Chores done, we dip fingers in bowls above the door,
bless ourselves with holy water, our house with song.

LEGEND

Your great uncle Patrick was
killed by the Black & Tan.

Familiar khaki, hooded, rifled.
Then a single *pop,* like a Judas-kiss.

Patrick's frailty, his years of endocarditis.
The poor infected heart, puffed out

with each beat, like frogs in mud.
At sixteen, he is propped up in bed

in the small cottage in Tramore
while his father helps a neighbor

paint a rowboat down the cove–
the police approach the water's edge,

almost friendly, asking: *what color*
you paintin' that boat, Martin?

And he, defiant, shouts back:
Any color but black & tan!

Imagine the mercenaries overnight,
their rage the next day when they come

upon the house, looking for Martin.
They study the list tacked behind

the cottage door: man-child, woman-child,
and find only sickly Patrick home.

They force him, in his cotton
bedclothes, sweaty, and collar-stained

against the poor fence post,
where years of hatred left

its splintery hairs upright:
a calico of wood resistance:

wooly sheep, poor burnt grass.
They don't shoot him, but

he dies nonetheless, fright
seizes his weak, boggy heart.

Nora, his mother wails and sways.
Thereafter, Martin drinks daily

in the newly blue boat: a hook for a fish,
burn of whiskey, torrid sun on water: guilt.

It is easier to call it an assassination,
to call it *legend* in our family.

But we know it was Martin's defiance
that did-in his fragile boy.

We need the story as a link back to place:
Patrick, our martyr, our necessary dead.

EVERYONE STANDS BENEATH THEIR OWN DOME OF HEAVEN

I stand in a field of nothing.
A dome of embossed paper all around me,
underneath my feet the rows of unplanned crops,
the seedless pockets of dirt, long hands of my family.
We are pre-everything,
the paper imprinted with the circle of fingertip,
the DNA of hair, and eye color, and sex.
This *heaven,* this *before separation.*
If we could make noise it would be joyous,
but it is only the beginning,
we are yet to name the animals and vines.
We are as reverent as serpents,
all these new connections of skin:
to be shed, left empty, inhabited, and shed again.

*

I would say something, but it is our
last day together and the whole forest
might burn down. All our kisses are tall
birch trees that crowd the clearing.
Paper bark peels back the pericardial sac.
Each branch pricks this thin membrane
of the heart, makes a hole where fluid
leaks out. What is left rubs raw.
The friction of leaving you in thicket.
Our arms on fire, our skin dry and ignitable.
To remember how once we were upside down
no easy way to distinguish your mouth

from mine. Outside then: magnolias
and Spanish moss. Now the woods are aflame.
If I glance back, I can see your ashy
outline across the lake.

*

They said the door was gold,
with rubies embedded in the handle
and a knocker of blue glass. *Hello?*
Hello? I called. On the other side:
hundreds of candles lit for the dead,
organ pipes measuring air and the faithful
on their knees in long pews.
I sneak into the confessional booth,
sins memorized, ready for forgiveness.
The small room gives way.
I land in a clearing of leaves...
I have moved into the body of a snake.
How could I ever have wanted arms and legs
when my belly moves me along so well.
My skin is jeweled and intricate.
All ideas are swallowed whole.
I have discovered the flexibility of my jaw.

*

Once I was a stupid field mouse:
dusty, with a long tail. My hands
were small claws, embarrassing really
the way I scurried after roaches
and grasshoppers. I nibbled the hard
casings of their bodies. Disgusted myself.
Then I ran into the mouth of a snake.

Its fangs shot out from behind the gum:
hollow funnels of bone. And the tongue:
the forked, venomous taste of it loved me.
I went blindly, drawn into its length.
The inside muscular and moist.
It was uncomplicated and rosy
to die like that: intact, carried off
into flesh and kept there.

SMALL FLIGHT TO DRILLING SITE, NEW MEXICO

I am the first one to notice the storm,
wide sky with a thick black cuff.
No one talks as we dip into rain, and the plane, foolishly
small now, rocks and drops, lightening on both sides of us
in frantic waves of otherwise beautiful blue light.

I start thinking of cows, because the men have clenched
their jaws against the erratic air and I will not be the only one
whimpering. I imagine I am patting the thick hard hide
of a cow, flies nested in its short hair. The cow loves me
with calm brown eyes. A big sunflower, a clown of a flower,
hangs behind him. Maybe I can do this: fall quietly to clay.
This excruciating silence is my faith, my deep
moo against turbulence. We drop.
Everyone closes their eyes. Quick. Tight.

When we level out, a rig worker says, *Jesus,*
cracks the *hush,* which was our testimony
and which we held on to for private reasons.

ORIGIN

The owl doesn't understand the genesis of feather.

Whose blueprint is this, planned deep swoop,
black shadow of wing and drop
that startles the mouse.

Later, bone and grizzle are regurgitated
in a berry-sized ball of fur,
a cottony *giving-back*
of all that was undigested, unused.

What blueprint then for me? Whose strategy
for how I live or who I love?
What frightens me: fire, water, the dark.

What do I carry uncradled in my gut?

JOHN

A wrenching:
the brother rises,
muscled and beautiful,
in the substantial arms of God.

HOUSE IN THE DREAM

If I take you hostage in the dream
and keep you locked in my house,
will I be able to enter the wide blue doors,
behind which fiddles can be heard?

If the house burns down and in slow motion
ash flutters from violins in the shape
of musical notes, and all the musicians have my face,
my bone structure, will *that* loosen the anguish

that is measured in the high beams of ceiling:
thick with decay and the weight of a flat roof,
snow packed against my tarred and feathered heart,
despair that is more about *his absence* than anything else.

JOHN,

The door ajar,
a bouquet of lilies.

Half of you falls away,
sky in place of shoulder.

POEMS OF CONFIDENCE FOR VALLEJO

Confianza...en el ala, no en el ave y en ti solo, en to solo, en ti solo.
—C. Vallejo

I

The wing is sculpted blue lead
and lays crushed on scorched earth.
All around it: hints of straw hair
and wax and cloth. The rounded wing
expands and contracts. It is too heavy
to ever leave the ground but it lives
with the knowledge of flight:
watch, before your eyes it spreads itself out,
everything else is backdrop for the wing
and the wing's life-long attempts
to take off from the black and steamy land.

II

I had looked so long at the chalky corpse:
curved white rib bone under skin,
the eyes dropped back behind the lid,
soft and colorless. I decided to love snakes
and spiders and all crawling earthly things.
I spent days watching the shifting ant hill
and the carrying off of crumbs.
If someone touched my skin it fell away
in pieces. I remembered there were windows
in the world and colored glass. I crushed
cobalt blue slivers, ground them into dust.
The wind made a stunning vapor for me and me alone.
I saw the leaf: painted and fallen against sand.
It had ribs and air and was singing.

JOHNNY

This simple pleasure of your name rising into the air behind my
head, and now for the first time I have the courage to say your
name, a daily prayer of your name, and your body rises in its
beautiful nineteen-year-old form. It occurs to me that soon you
will be dead longer than you were living, this strange torture
settles in the layer of air between dermis and epidermis,
the space between dura and subdura, the hair follicle and the hair
shaft, each part with its own name, like us, the function
of each dependent on the other, and like us, the air minimal,
an inconsequential space. Johnny in the spring day on Erie Street,
leaps to catch the ball, his jacket billows out with free breath,
in just two weeks we will know the beginning of terror
and the useless flexibility of spine and knee joint when we
kneel to pray for you. The absolute uselessness of what we
want it to be or what we *need it to be,* the dreaded roller
coaster of your illness where we are locked in the front seat, our
arms in the rapid air, screaming. Johnny of the long curved
back and leg, what was I thinking when I let go of you,
the dark scarf of death so tight around you, I should have gone
myself into the cave where you were seeking air, and held your
hand again and worked the linen from your neck until
you broke free. Johnny of the first half of my life and childhood
of my life and all the early rooms of my life, how ridiculous
to be remembering you with this solemn repetition while
outside the wolf-dog leaps in the leaves, and in the oven
Christmas bread widens and rises.

NOTES

"Bat Box" is after a sculpture by Chris Romer.

"Imagine Your Face Is in a Melon" is after a photo by Emmy Perez.

"Justifiable Circles" is after a sculpture by Didier Corallo.

"Everyone Stands Beneath Their Own Dome of Heaven" is a variation on the title of a painting by Anselm Kiefer.

Section quotes are all from *The Cistercian World: Monastic Writings of the Twelfth Century.* Trans. Paul Matarasso. New York: Penguin Books, 1993.

Epigraph for "The Illustrious Providence of Solid Tumors" from *Narratives of the Witchcraft Cases 1648-1706.*
Ed. George L. Burr. New York: Barnes & Noble, Inc., 1952.

Mary Jane Nealon is a registered nurse, poet, and freelance medical writer. She is a graduate of the Warren Wilson College MFA Program for Writers. She is the recipient of two fellowships from the Fine Arts Work Center in Provincetown, Massachusettes, 1995-1997. In 1998, she was awarded a fellowship from the New Jersey State Council on the Arts and the Mid-Atlantic Arts Foundation. She lives in Jersey City, New Jersey.